Old BUCKIE

by
Iain Sinclair

BUCKIE FROM CRAIGBO

A panoramic view of the rooftops of Buckie taken from Craigbo, to the south of the town.

First published in the United Kingdom, 2000,
by Stenlake Publishing Ltd.
54–58 Mill Square,
Catrine, Ayrshire KA5 6RD
Telephone: 01290 551122
www.stenlake.co.uk

ISBN 1 84033 096 1

The publishers regret that they cannot supply
copies of any pictures featured in this book.

ACKNOWLEDGMENTS

I am grateful to Bill Murray and his Uncle Willie for a splendid
evening of memories conjured up by these pictures, and to Bill
for reviewing my notes.

The United Free Church (South Church) is the final member of
the trio of fine churches in Buckie. The children in the
foreground, all in their Sunday best, were possibly members of
the Sunday school, assembled specially for this photograph.

INTRODUCTION

Situated on the Moray Firth coastline, Buckie lies some seventeen miles east of Elgin and 70 miles north-west of Aberdeen. It was the largest town in the old county of Banffshire, and in the later part of the nineteenth century consisted of three main divisions: Buckpool, Easter Buckie, and Portessie (Nether Buckie, to the west of the Buckie Burn dates from about 1650, and Easter Buckie, east of the burn from 1723). Buckie, Buckpool and the communities of Ianstown and Gordonsburgh were created a burgh in 1888, and Portessie was incorporated into the burgh in 1903.

The activities of Buckie centre largely round Cluny Harbour, named after local landowner Mr Gordon of Cluny. He built the original harbour – consisting of two basins and covering an area of eight acres – in 1880, later handing the rights to a Board of Trustees and Commissioners who further expanded it. It was eventually purchased by the town council and remains under the control of the local authority to this day.

Buckie's prosperity was built on the herring trade in the nineteenth century, and to take advantage of that growing prosperity the Highland Railway opened a branch line from Keith to Buckie in 1884. Two years later the Great North of Scotland Railway finished the extension of their line from Aberdeen to Elgin, completing a connecting link for the carrying on of commerce and convenience of the travelling public. Alas, today the herring trade has gone, as have the two rail connections.

Lying in a sheltered bay between the headlands of Lossiemouth and Portknockie, Buckie provided many facilities for the visitor, with two excellent golf courses, pleasant beaches and an open-air swimming pool at Strathlene. This pool, formerly administered by Buckie Town Council, is now closed and boarded up, and has been left to the mercy of the elements. Adjacent to the pool stood the imposing Strathlene Hotel, now converted to flats.

No visitor to Buckie can fail to be impressed by it imposing churches. Conspicuous among these are the twin spires of St Peter's Roman Catholic Church, opened in 1857. These spires rise to a height of 115 feet and form a notable local architectural feature. The former Established Church, now known as the North Church, stands overlooking East Church Street and Cluny Square. It took two years to construct, cost £4,000, and was opened in 1880. The town's clock, a generous gift of the late Mr Donaldson, baker, is situated in the tower.

Other buildings worthy of architectural comment are the original public school (now flats) and the Fishermen's Hall. On a modern note there is now a splendid memorial chapel located on the west side of the town, built by subscriptions from the town's fishermen, and dedicated to the memory of those who lost their lives at sea.

Many of the substantial dwelling houses in Buckie reflect the prosperity derived from the herring trade. Herring fishing led to the growth of other industries, and Buckie also boasted engineering works, barrel makers, net and sail makers, chandleries, fish processors and three shipyards.

The fishing fleet has shrunk considerably but Buckie still supports two large fish processors, a shipyard (an amalgamation of Herd and MacKenzie Ltd. and Jones (Buckie) Shipyard Ltd.) and a large maltings associated with the whisky trade for which neighbouring Speyside is famous.

Pupils and teachers of the old Free Church School – 'The Townie School' – photographed in 1870 by W. F. Johnston and Sons, the present publishers of the *Banffshire Advertiser*, or 'Buckie Squeak' as it is affectionately known.

North Pringle Street, photographed *c*.1906 from its junction with West Church Street. The Church of Christ and the Fishermen's Hall are on the left. The hall was built with stone from Hopeman, and was funded entirely by the fishermen themselves. The bridge in the middle distance carried the road over the Aberdeen to Elgin railway line, a victim of the Beeching cuts in 1968.

WEST CATHCART STREET, BUCKIE

West Cathcart Street, showing different styles of housing. Terraced houses built at the turn of the century face straight on to the street, while the more modern semi-detached bungalows opposite include front and rear gardens. The tower of the South Church, at the corner of East Cathcart Street and High Street, stands in the distance.

5

Cliff Terrace, Buckie.

Cliff Terrace has a splendid view of the harbour, Moray Firth and beyond, and many of its substantial sandstone dwellings originally belonged to well-to-do fish merchants. One of the leading lights, situated to help vessels enter Buckie Harbour safely, is just visible on the left of the picture.

The houses of Mill Crescent were built in the inter-war years by the local authority to accommodate Buckie's growing population. This increase in population was largely due to the prosperity that fishing had brought to the area. By 1950, however, Buckie had started to decline as a white fish port, and to counteract this and to qualify under the Distribution of Industry Act, the town council pressed for Buckie to be scheduled as a development area. The idea was to attract new industry to the town to offset its heavy dependence on fishing, and as a result of this AEI set up a light bulb factory in the town.

The first harbour in the Buckie area was situated at Buckpool (above). There was also a harbour at the Hythe and a natural bay at the Yardie, where fishing boats were dragged ashore when not in use. In 1843 a wooden harbour was erected at the Hythe, but within six years this had been washed away. The harbour at Buckpool (Nether Buckie) was built in 1857. It was never very satisfactory, being exposed to north-easterly gales, and this prompted John Gordon of Cluny to build Cluny Harbour, which was completed in 1878 at a cost of £65,000. This picture looks towards the Seatown of Buckie where fishermen's cottages are still in evidence today. The vessel in the foreground is a scaffie, identified with the Moray area and having a rounded bow and raked stern. The smaller boat alongside the harbour wall is a Fifie, characterised by vertical bow and stern posts and having its origins in Fife. The men on the pier are dressed in traditional fishermen's clothing.

8

As there was insufficient room for harbouring all the boats at the Seatown, many were beached on the shore at high tide. This was also common practice in the winter when the weather turned bad. The gasometer stored the town's gas supply, which before the days of North Sea gas was produced locally from coal. Tar was a by-product of coal gas, and was used to treat fishing ropes and nets.

The west end of Buckie, photographed in 1907. The large building in the middle distance on the left was a granary. To the right of railway line (the main line from Aberdeen to Elgin) lies Gibbs Brae and the Athol Inn, renowned for only serving beer.

The community of Ianstown lies at the east end of Buckie. McLarens Brae occupies the foreground of this picture, and the fencing along it would have been put to good use as a place to hang fishing nets out to dry. The substantial sawmill beyond the railway line was destroyed by fire in 1930. Herd & MacKenzie's boatyard, known locally as Herdies, and famous for building fishing vessels and the three-mast schooner the *Captain Scott*, occupies the site where the boat is beached.

IANSTOWN - LOOKING EAST

IANSTON, BUCKIE

A photograph of Ianstown taken in 1926 showing fishermen's houses with neatly-painted stonework around the windows. The smokestack at the rear right of belonged to Jones Shipyard in Buckie. The yard didn't stand within the harbour limits and instead its slipway launched vessels directly into the open sea.

The sands at Strathlene, looking to the east of the bay. Strathlene House, the home of the Earl of Seafield's factor, latterly became a very comfortable hotel and has now been converted into flats. The open-air swimming pool (now closed) is located behind Strathlene House, while the start of Strathlene Golf Course, with its splendid views over the Moray Firth, lies to the right. There was once a salmon station located on the foreshore at Strathlene, where cobles, the small boats used for salmon fishing, and posts for drying nets, could be seen.

Cairnfield House, Buckie.

Cairnfield was the ancestral home of the Gordons of Cairnfield until around 1980. An earlier house on the site was destroyed by fire in 1798 and the present building (shown in the picture), dating from 1802, was designed by Robert Burn of Edinburgh. The west wing was added in 1825. A further addition in 1930, now used as the kitchen, was probably originally intended as a library.

14

This building stands at the north side of Cluny Square. The photograph, dated 1905, shows the premises of L. T. McGarth, traditional ironmongers, who also sold china and glassware. To the rear of the building at the left hand side was Menzies barber's shop. The property is currently occupied by a building society and dry cleaners.

BOWLING GREEN & TENNIS COURT BUCKIE

Looking down from the tower of the North Church in Cluny Square to the bowling green and tennis court in 1907. The green still flourishes today but the tennis courts have long gone. Fishing boats are under construction at George Smith's shipyard, which later became the site of a diesel powered electricity generating station for the town. When that closed George Thomson & Sons yard took over the site. Vessels built in the yard were launched directly into the Moray Firth off the beach. The yard finally closed in the mid-1980s and the town's two remaining yards amalgamated in 1991.

The dedication of the War Memorial in Cluny Square in 1925 with a full parade of soldiers and a very large turnout of locals. Judging by the sea of flat caps in the foreground it would appear that the crowd was largely male. From right to left the buildings in the background were the premises of Tindall the ironmonger, offices of John Layton Smith, solicitor and town clerk, and Esson men's outfitters. The building on the left is now the premises of the Clydesdale Bank.

CRAIGMIN BRIDGE, BUCKIE

97685 (JV)

The strange-looking Craigmin Bridge spans the Buckie Burn at Drybridge, some two miles from Buckie. The photograph suggests that a second bridge was built on top of the first, and this may indeed have been the case. It is said that the original approaches to the bridge were too steep for horse-drawn traffic, and that to overcome this a further level was added.

Heading west out of Buckie towards Buckpool along West Church Street, one crosses the fine Victoria Bridge over the Buckie Burn. The original bridge was swept away in a spate in 1829 and the present stone structure erected thereafter. The coat of arms of the Burgh of Buckie has a traditional fishing craft as the main feature. The coat of arms can be seen carved into the stonework of the gable end of first house in Queen Street, facing onto West Church Street. Queen Street was once described by people in Buckie as the place where 'granders' lived!

218586.

THE SQUARE AND NORTH CHURCH, BUCKIE.

Cluny Square showing the War Memorial at the junction of the four roads leading into the square. The memorial was moved some years ago, and now stands on the pedestrian area at the left of the picture. A hall complex has now been added to the side and rear of the North Church. The manse stands to the right of the church.

THE SQUARE, BUCKIE

B 9418

Looking towards the High Street from the north side of Cluny Square, with the spire of the South Church in the distance. Replica wartime mines, painted bright red, were a feature of many coastal towns and villages after the Second World War, and were used as collection boxes for donations to the Shipwrecked Mariners Society.

Looking east from the tower of the North Church. Old Buckie High School, now flats, is just visible on the far left of the picture; to the right in the foreground is the West Church (latterly a community centre); the Episcopal Church and manse; and Dr Duguid's house (now an Abbeyside residential home). The row of terraced houses in the middle distance on the extreme right were formerly coastguard houses.

High Street, Buckie. 11.

The building at the end of the street on the left was originally Stephens Temperance Hotel, then housed a dental surgery, and is now the Cluny Hotel. To the right, under the awnings, stands a branch of that well-known grocery chain, Liptons, with its delivery van at the door.

HIGH STREET, BUCKIE

Substantial stone houses at the upper end of High Street, evidence of the wealth that fishing brought to Buckie at the turn of the century.

East Church Street from the tower of the North Church. To the left of the picture one can just pick out the slipway of Herd & MacKenzie Ltd. and beyond that the slipway of Jones (Buckie) Shipyard. Both these yards had an impressive history of boat-building in the twentieth century, and amalgamated in 1991. Though there are far fewer fishing vessels now being built, the combined yards, trading under the name of Buckie Shipyards Ltd., carry out a diverse range of work from boat repairs to RNLI lifeboat servicing. Housing in Mill Crescent, Linn Crescent, and Well Road, to the right of the picture, has started to be built.

Looking along East Church Street at the beginning of the twentieth century. The gentleman on the left is wearing traditional fishermen's garb. Watson's grocery store and the Globe Stores are to the right.

EAST CHURCH STREET, BUCKIE.

B.238.

A quiet view of East Church Street, looking in the opposite direction from the previous picture, and reproduced from a postcard sent in 1951. The principal shops to the right are MacKay's the draper, along with the chemists and Milne's newsagents.

East Church Street showing the fine building occupied by the Bank of Scotland to the right, and Logie's Steps leading to the harbour area via the station. The steps took their name from a firm of chandlers who were located at the bottom of them.

With the Seasons Greetings .... Church Street, E., Buckie

This view of a deserted East Church Street was taken in 1910 and used as a Christmas card, although there isn't a robin or piece of holly in sight. It must have been a sunny day as the canopies are down shading the display windows of MacKay's drapers shop.

East Church Street. Buckie

Although the businesses have changed, these fine buildings remain very much as they were in 1931. The cottage-type house with dormer windows has been demolished, however, and new larger shop premises now occupy the site.

Three of the town's churches dominate this picture: the Episcopal Church, the West Kirk and St Peter's Roman Catholic Church. The building to the left was occupied by the Seamen's Home, one of a number of such homes found in all the major fishing ports where fishermen were able to get a bed, washing facilities and a meal. Most of these are now closed due to better facilities on board vessels, and the fact that fishermen can travel home at weekends from distant ports.

In this closer view several well-known features of the town can be identified: the Seamen's Home to the left, the volunteer hall, the cinema and Fowler's the baker. Alas, none of these survive today.

The railings outside the houses were removed during the Second World War to help the war effort, and the tower of the former school (now flats) has been dismantled since this pre-First World War picture was taken.

This picture of the railway station features on a postcard sent in 1904. A variety of craft are in the harbour, although commercial rather than fishing vessels tended to use this basin. The left basin acted as a spending beach to dissipate wave-energy as the sea flowed in the harbour mouth, and has now been filled in. The railway from Elgin via the coast was of major importance to the fishing industry and provided both goods and passenger links to Aberdeen and the south. There was also a branch line to Keith. Alas, the Beeching cuts led to the closure of this line in 1968.

The Harbour, Buckie

This picture, with herring barrels loaded on to wagons and standing on the quayside, amply demonstrates the importance of the railway to the economy of the town. Buckie was originally lit by gas lighting, and the lamp in the picture can't have provided much illumination. GNS on the wagon denotes the Great North of Scotland Railway.

The Harbour, Buckie.

BURGH · OF · BUCKIE

RELIABLE WR&S SERIES

A harbour supports a variety of services from shipbuilding and engineering to fishing and chandlery businesses, and Buckie did and still does have all of these components of a fishing port. Although trade today is significantly smaller than in the past, the town nevertheless still supports a reasonable commercial traffic. One local industry is the malting of barley for the whisky distilleries in the Spey valley. This picture dates from *c*.1907, following which the harbour was extended with a longer breakwater extending into the Moray Firth. The town's coat of arms usually includes the date 1888 on the boat's sails – the date Buckie became a police burgh. The rooftop in the immediate foreground is that of the signal box for the railway through Buckie.

This postcard is captioned 'The first in', which for the fishing boat concerned meant arriving first at the fish market and hopefully getting the best price for its catch. This Zulu is typical of the vessels that would have crowded the harbour in the early part of the twentieth century. The crew had little shelter against the elements and there was no hydraulic machinery to assist in the hauling of the nets. Initially Zulus were powered by sail only. Most were eventually converted to motor power with the manufacturers Kelvin, Gardner and Gleniffer supplying the majority of the engines.

Cluny Harbour, Buckie

RELIABLE WR&S SERIES 970

A busy scene in the harbour with boats lying alongside the quays. Worthy of note are the wooden fenders which were used before tyres became available as an alternative. Neatly stowed to the right on the spar are the various nets, ropes and dog buoys (so-called because they were allegedly made from the skins of dead dogs) that formed part of the day-to-day gear on board the vessels.

Long-line fishing vessels lying alongside the harbour in 1905. The style and type of fishing boats changed as sail gave way to steam and latterly diesel power. Wheelhouses and cabin accommodation were later additions. These vessels bear the BF (Banff) registration, used by local vessels before Buckie became a registration port in its own right.

THE HARBOUR, BUCKIE

Drifters berthed side by side nose up against the quay wall. Boats were frequently so tightly-packed in the harbour that it was possible to walk across it by stepping from deck to deck. The triangular structure in the background is a set of sheerlegs, used to lift heavy pieces of equipment such as boilers onto vessels by means of a hand winch.

S.S. "PRIMROSE BAY" PORTKNOCKIE.

The *Primrose Bay* was a typical steam drifter with its large funnel, wheelhouse and open deck. She was from Portknockie, but was registered PD (Peterhead). Alas, there are no surviving examples of the steam drifters today, and although attempts were made a few years ago to restore and preserve one, their story has been consigned to the history books.

CLUNY HARBOUR, BUCKIE

Following the era of the steam drifters, seine netters, with their neat lines and wooden construction, dominated the fishing industry. They had limited deck machinery and as this picture shows a large fleet operated out of Buckie. To the rear are the fine bungalows of Cliff Terrace which command excellent views across the Moray Firth.

42

BUCKIE HARBOUR

D 1543

Featuring fewer boats, this later photograph shows the beginning of the decline in the fishing industry. In the centre, behind the BCK (Buckie) registered boat, is the Fishery Protection vessel, operated by the Department of Agriculture and Fisheries for Scotland and very important in today's climate of quotas, restricted net sizes and widespread fishing by foreign vessels.

The herring trade not only brought prosperity to Buckie and its fishermen, but also provided work for the large number of girls who gutted, salted and packed the fish for export. As the shoals moved to other waters around Britain, the girls travelled with the fleet to ports in England and the Isle of Man.

Scotch Fishwives.

Wearing traditional fishwives' dress, these ladies, each armed with a creel (wicker basket) of fish, would travel to surrounding villages to sell the catch.

Cod Fishing at Lossiemouth.
A Record Day's Catch.

A fine catch of cod laid out on the quayside for sale. Cod were sold by the score and the picture shows a fishwife with her creel, selecting fish for selling. Although this picture was taken at Lossiemouth, similar scenes were once common in Buckie too.

Portessie, looking East

73540.

The small village of Portessie, with its neat fishermen's cottages, gable end to the sea, lies to the east of Buckie. This picture predates the building of the road to Findochty and Portknockie along the front.

Portessie was originally a small fishing village in its own right, the line of the village following the natural line of the bay. Cottages were built with their gable ends to the sea to protect them from the worst of the weather in stormy conditions.